ED 12808

Mainz · London · Madrid · New York · Paris · Prague · Tokyo · Toronto

ED 12808
British Library Cataloguing-in-Publication Data.
A catalogue record for this book is available from the British Library
ISBN 1-902455-12-6
ISMN M-2201-2294-1

Illustrations by John Minnion
Design and typesetting by adamhaystudio.com
Music setting by Enigma Music Production Services
Printed in Germany S&Co.7897

Contents

1. Away in a Manger

Music: William James Kirkpatrick (1838–1921)
Words: Anonymous, Philadelphia 1883
Arr. Barrie Carson Turner

Slowly

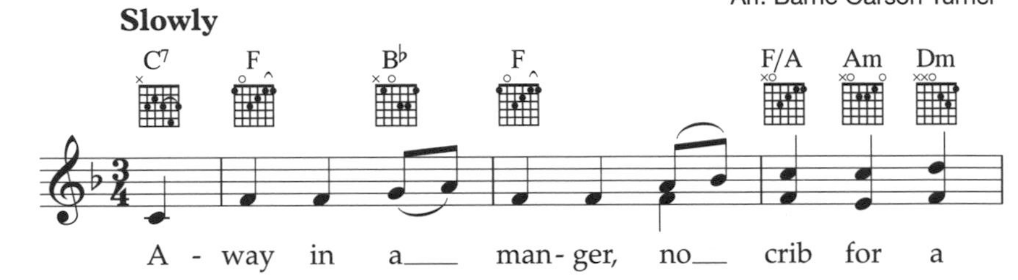

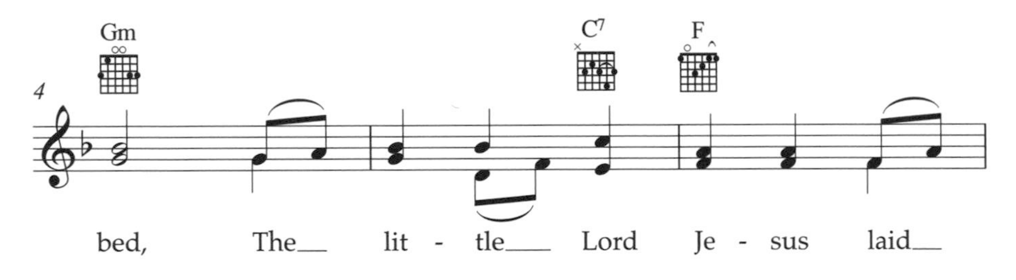

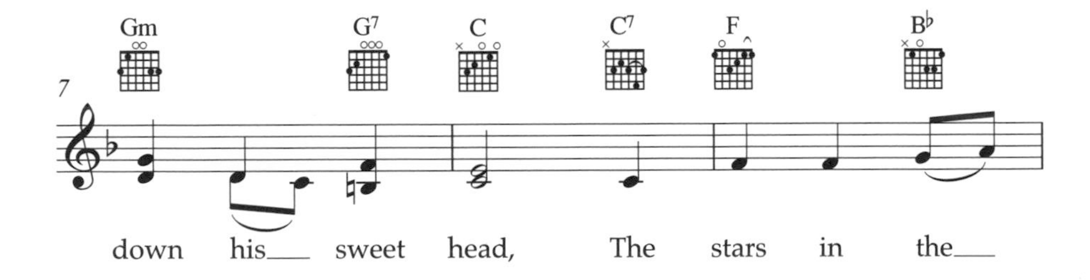

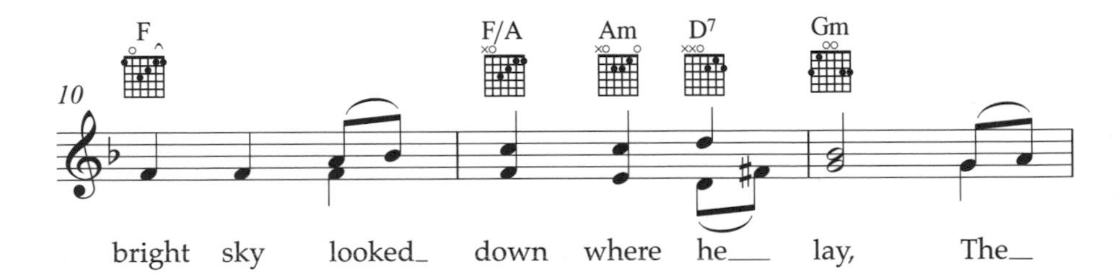

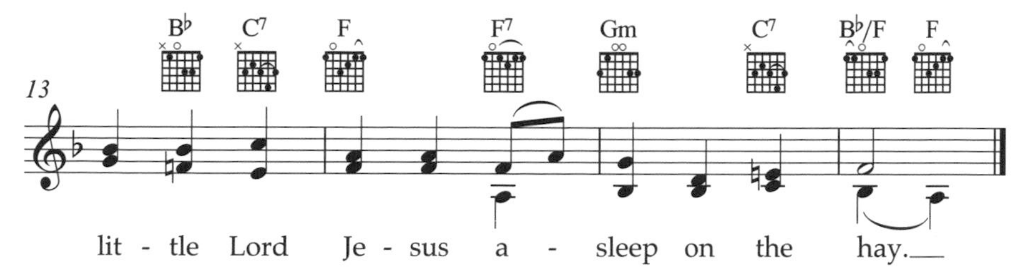

2. The cattle are lowing, the baby awakes,
   But little Lord Jesus no crying he makes.
   I love thee, Lord Jesus! Look down from the sky,
   And stay by my side until morning is nigh.

3. Be near me, Lord Jesus; I ask thee to stay
   Close by me for ever, and love me, I pray.
   Bless all the dear children in thy tender care,
   And fit us for heaven, to live with thee there.

2. As with Gladness Men of Old

Music: Adapted from a chorale, *Treuer Heiland*,
by Conrad Kocher (1786–1872)
Words: William Chatterton Dix (1837–98)
Arr. Barrie Carson Turner

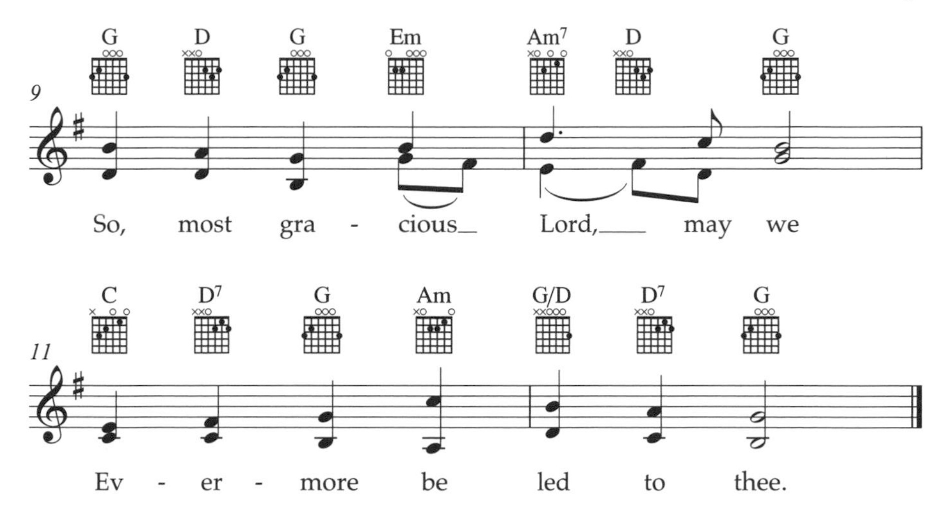

2. As with joyful steps they sped,
To that lowly manger-bed,
There to bend the knee before
Thee, whom heaven and earth adore:
So may we with willing feet
Ever seek thy mercy-seat.

3. As they offered gifts most rare
At that manger rude and bare,
So may we with holy joy,
Pure, and free from sin's alloy,
All our costliest treasures bring,
Christ, to thee, our heavenly King.

4. Holy Jesus, every day
Keep us in the narrow way;
And, when earthly things are past,
Bring our ransomed souls at last
Where they need no star to guide,
Where no clouds thy glory hide.

5. In the heavenly country bright
Need they no created light;
Thou its light, its joy, its crown,
Thou its sun which goes not down;
There for ever may we sing
Hallelujahs to our King.

3. Hark! The Herald Angels Sing

Music: Felix Mendelssohn (1809–47)
From *Festgesang* (1840)
Words: Charles Wesley (1707–88) and others
Arr. Barrie Carson Turner

Moderately fast

G D7 G G/D D G/B C

Hark! the he - rald an - gels sing_ Glo - ry to the

4

G/D D7 G G Em B7 Em A7

new - born King. Peace on earth and mer - cy mild,_

7

D/F♯ G D/A A7 Dsus D G/B D7/F♯ G G/D D

God and sin - ners re - con - ciled: Joy - ful all ye na - tions rise,_

11

G/B D7 G G/D G7 C C+ E7

Join the tri - umph of the skies,_ With th'an - gel - ic

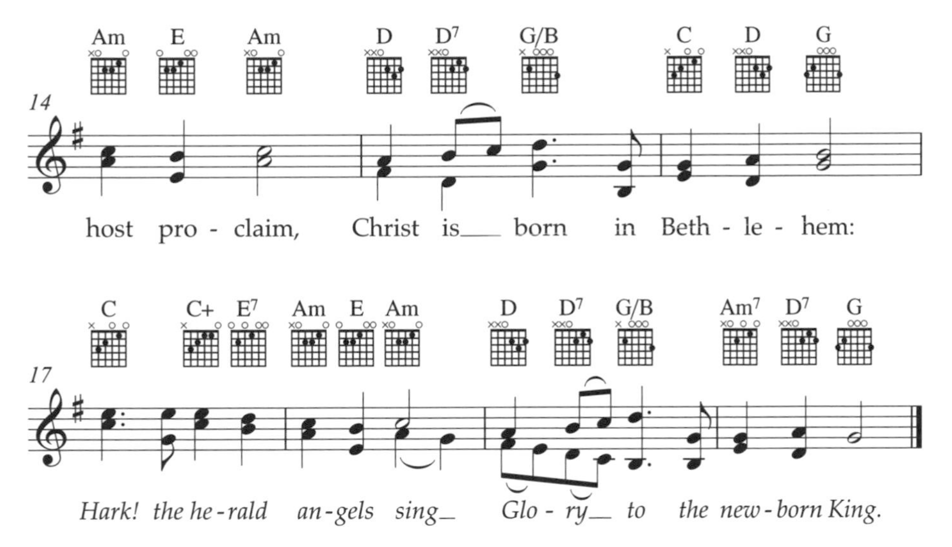

2. Christ, by highest heaven adored,
   Christ, the everlasting Lord,
   Late in time behold him come
   Offspring of a Virgin's womb!
   Veiled in flesh the Godhead see,
   Hail the incarnate Deity!
   Pleased as man with man to dwell,
   Jesus, our Emmanuel:
   Hark! the herald angels sing
   Glory to the new-born King.

3. Hail the heaven-born Prince of peace!
   Hail the Sun of Righteousness!
   Light and life to all he brings,
   Risen with healing in his wings;
   Mild he lays his glory by,
   Born that man no more may die,
   Born to raise the sons of earth,
   Born to give them second birth:

4. A Virgin Most Pure

Words and Music: English traditional
Arr. Barrie Carson Turner

Moderately

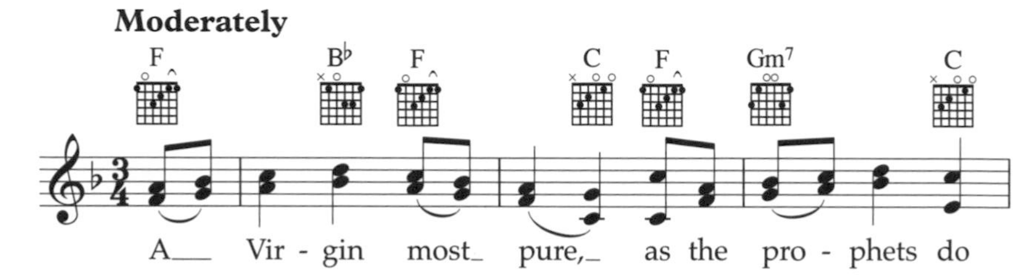

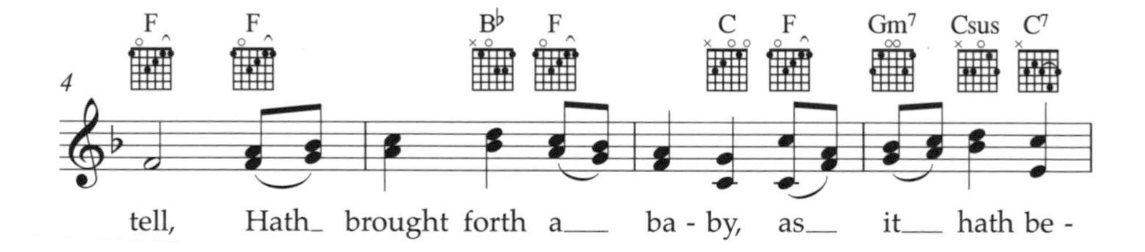

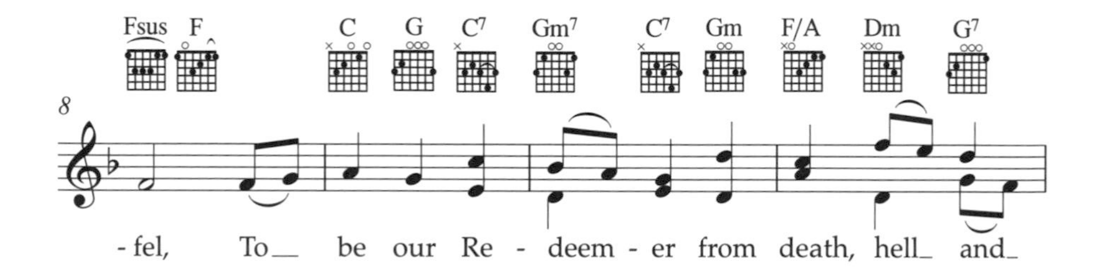

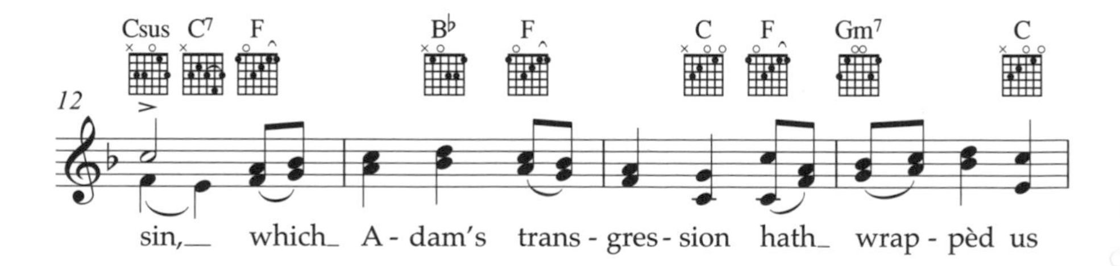

2. At Bethlem in Jewry a city there was
Where Joseph and Mary together did pass,
All for to be taxèd with many one moe,
For Caesar commanded the same should be so.

And therefore be merry, set sorrow aside;
Christ Jesus our Saviour was born on this tide.

3. But when they had entered the city so fair,
A number of people so mighty was there,
That Joseph and Mary, whose substance was small,
Could find in the inn there no lodging at all.

4. Then were they constrainèd in a stable to lie,
Where horses and asses they used for to tie;
Their lodging so simple they took it no scorn,
But against the next morning our Saviour was born.

5. The King of all kings to this world being brought,
Small store of fine linen to wrap him was sought,
But when she had swaddled her young son so sweet,
Within an ox-manger she laid him to sleep.

6. Then God sent an angel from heaven so high
To certain poor shepherds in fields where they lie,
And bade them no longer in sorrow to stay,
Because that our Saviour was born on this day.

7. Then presently after the shepherds did spy
A number of angels that stood in the sky;
They joyfully talkèd and sweetly did sing,
To God be all glory, our heavenly King.

5. It Came Upon the Midnight Clear

Music: English traditional, adapted by Arthur Sullivan (1842–1900)
Words: Edmund Hamilton Sears (1810–76)
Arr. Barrie Carson Turner

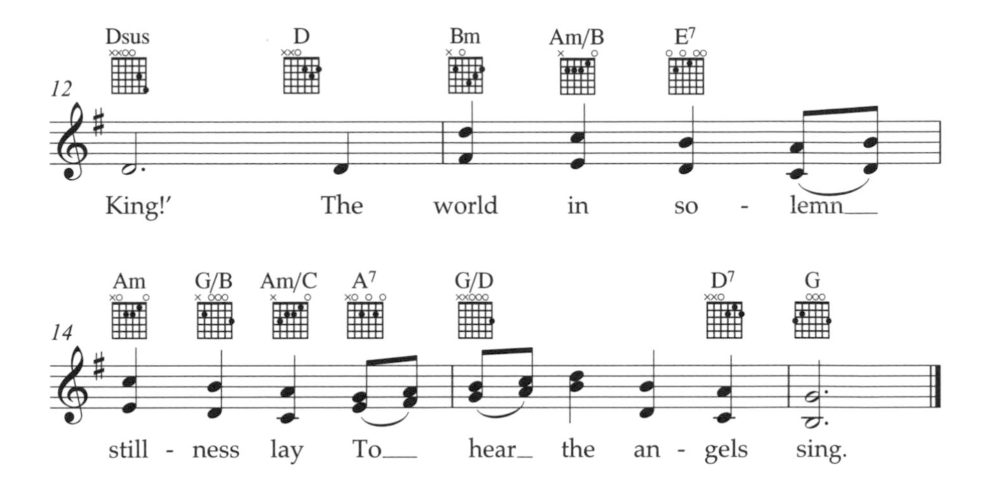

2. Still through the cloven skies they come,
 With peaceful wings unfurled;
 And still their heavenly music floats
 O'er all the weary world;
 Above its sad and lowly plains
 They bend on hovering wing,
 And ever o'er its Babel–sounds
 The blessèd angels sing.

3. Yet with the woes of sin and strife
 The world has suffered long;
 Beneath the angel-strain have rolled
 Two thousand years of wrong;
 And man, at war with man, hears not
 The love-song which they bring:
 O hush the noise, ye men of strife,
 And hear the angels sing!

4. For lo! the days are hastening on,
 By prophet-bards foretold,
 When, with the ever-circling years
 Comes round the age of gold;
 When peace shall over all the earth
 Its ancient splendours fling,
 And the whole world give back the song
 Which now the angels sing.

6. Christians, Awake, Salute the Happy Morn

Music: J. Wainwright (1723–68)
Words: John Byrom (1691–1763)
Arr. Barrie Carson Turner

Joyful and bright

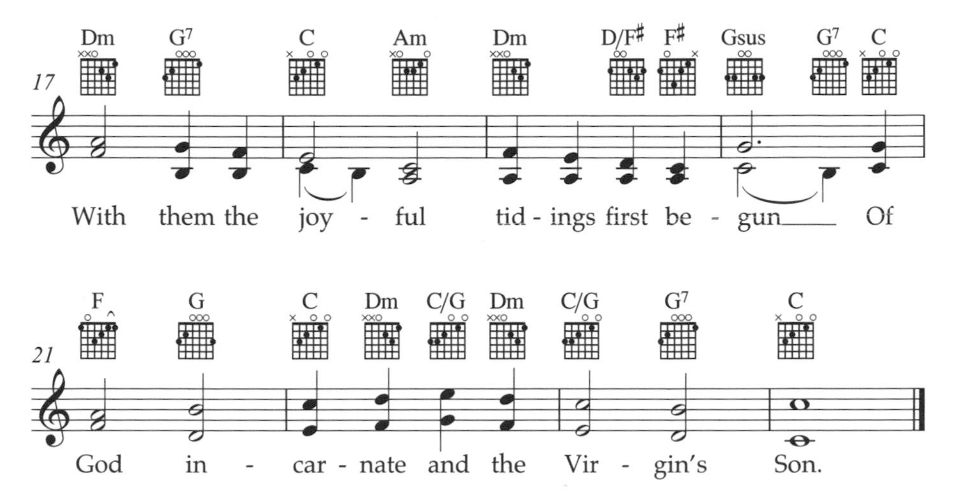

2. Then to the watchful shepherds it was told,
Who heard th'angelic herald's voice: 'Behold,
I bring good tidings of a Saviour's birth
To you and all the nations upon earth;
This day has God fulfilled his promised word,
This day is born a Saviour, Christ the Lord.'

3. He spake; and straightway the celestial choir
In hymns of joy, unknown before, conspire.
The praises of redeeming love they sang,
And heav'n's whole orb with alleluias rang;
God's highest glory was their anthem still,
Peace upon earth, and unto men goodwill.

4. O may we keep and ponder in our mind
God's wondrous love in saving lost mankind;
Trace we the babe, who hath retrieved our loss,
From the poor manger to the bitter cross;
Tread in his steps, assisted by his grace,
Till man's first heav'nly state again takes place.

5. Then may we hope, the angelic hosts among,
To sing, redeemed, a glad triumphal song;
He that was born upon this joyful day
Around us all his glory shall display;
Saved by his love, incessant we shall sing
Eternal praise to heav'n's almighty King.

7. This Endris Night

Words and Melody: English, 15th century
Arr. Barrie Carson Turner

*this endris night = a few nights ago
**skill = reasonable, fitting

2. This virgin clear withouten fear,
   Unto her Son gan say,
   'My Son, my Lord, my Father dere,
   Why liest thou in hay?'

3. Now my sweet Son, since it is so,
   All things are at thy will,
   Grant me I pray this boon today
   If it be right and **skill.

4. That child or man that will or can
   Be merry upon my day
   To bliss him bring, and I shall sing,
   'Lullay, lullay, lullay'.

8. Once in Royal David's City

Music: Henry John Gauntlett (1805–76)
Words: Cecil Frances Alexander (1818–95)
Arr. Barrie Carson Turner

2. He came down to earth from heaven
   Who is God and Lord of all,
   And his shelter was a stable,
   And his cradle was a stall:
   With the poor and mean and lowly,
   Lived on earth our Saviour holy.

3. And through all his wondrous childhood
   He would honour and obey,
   Love and watch the lowly Maiden,
   In whose gentle arms he lay:
   Christian children all must be
   Mild, obedient, good as he.

4. For he is our childhood's pattern,
   Day by day like us he grew,
   He was little, weak, and helpless,
   Tears and smiles like us he knew;
   And he feeleth for our sadness,
   And he shareth in our gladness.

5. And our eyes at last shall see him,
   Through his own redeeming love,
   For that child so dear and gentle
   Is our Lord in heaven above;
   And he leads his children on
   To the place where he is gone.

6. Not in that poor lowly stable,
   With the oxen standing by,
   We shall see him; but in heaven,
   Set at God's right hand on high;
   Where like stars his children crowned
   All in white shall wait around.

9. Child in the Manger

(Leanabh an Aigh)

Music: Celtic traditional carol
Words: Mary Macdonald (1817–90)
Translation by: Lachlan Macbean (1853–1931)
Arr. Barrie Carson Turner

Gently, with a lilt

2. Once the most holy
   Child of salvation,
   Gently and lowly,
   Lived below;
   Now, as our glorious
   Mighty Redeemer,
   See him victorious
   O'er each foe.

3. Prophets foretold him,
   Infant of wonder;
   Angels behold him
   On his throne;
   Worthy our Saviour
   Of all their praises;
   Happy for ever
   Are his own.

10. The First Nowell

Words and Music: English traditional
arr. John Stainer (1840–1901)
Arr. Barrie Carson Turner

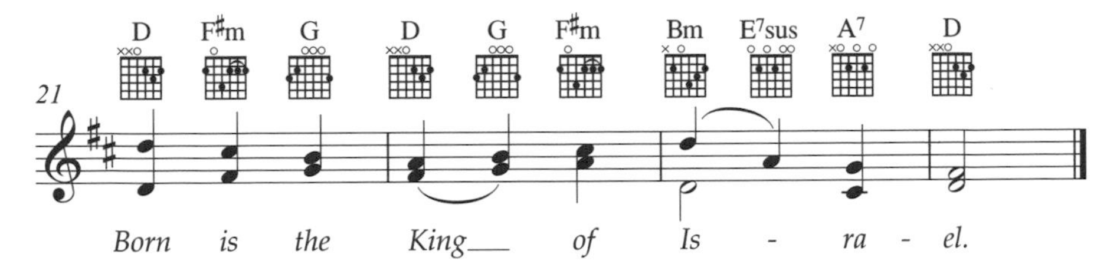

2. They lookèd up and saw a star,
   Shining in the east, beyond them far:
   And to the earth it gave great light,
   And so it continued both day and night:
   Nowell, Nowell, Nowell, Nowell,
   Born is the King of Israel.

3. And by the light of that same star,
   Three Wise Men came from country far;
   To seek for a king was their intent,
   And to follow the star wherever it went:

4. This star drew nigh to the north-west;
   O'er Bethlehem it took its rest,
   And there it did both stop and stay
   Right over the place where Jesus lay:

5. Then entered in those Wise Men three,
   Fell reverently upon their knee,
   And offered there in his presènce
   Their gold and myrrh and frankincense:

6. Then let us all with one accord
   Sing praises to our heavenly Lord,
   That hath made heaven and earth of naught,
   And with his blood mankind hath bought:

11. Deck the Hall

(Nos Galan)

Music: Welsh traditional carol
Words: traditional
Arr. Barrie Carson Turner

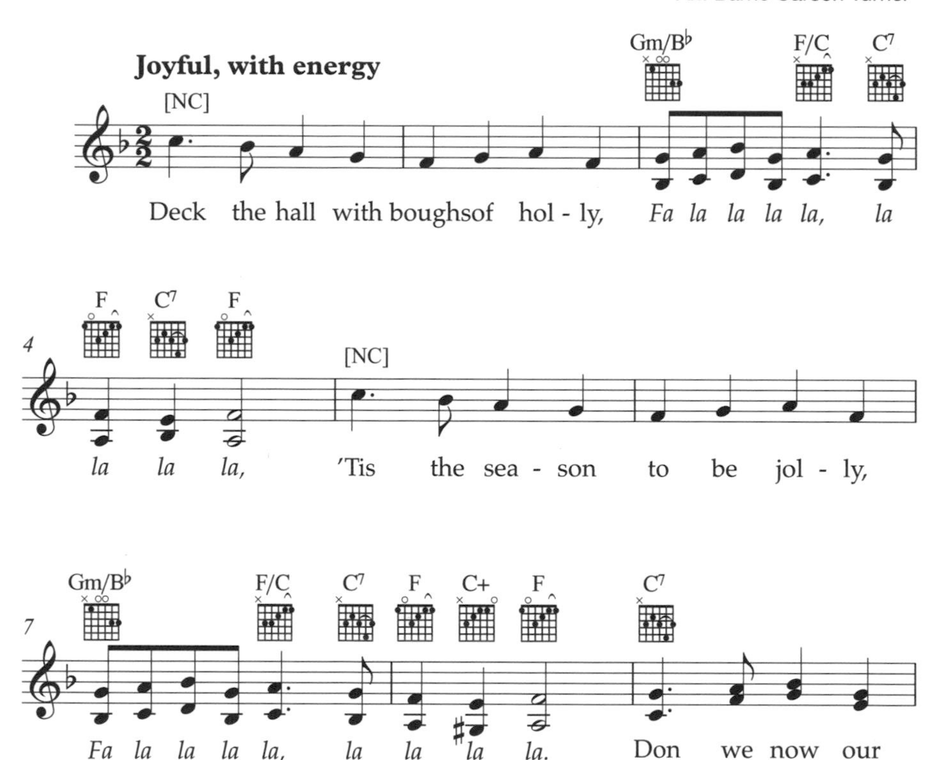

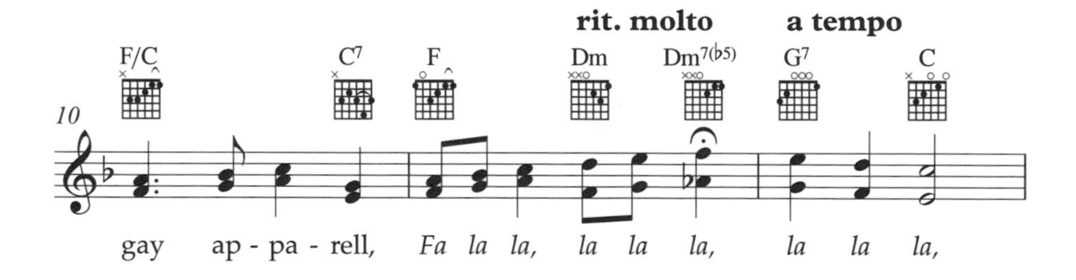

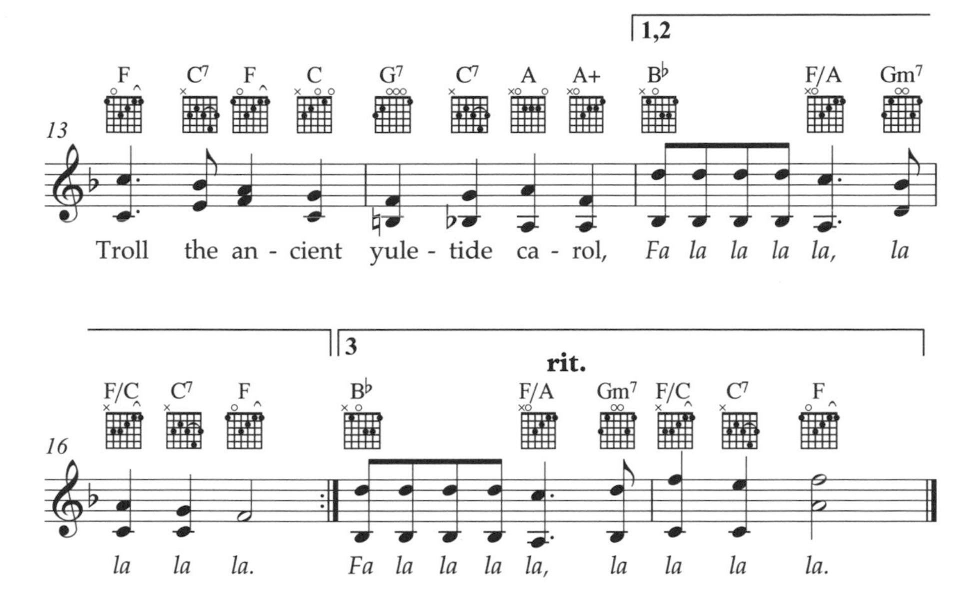

2. See the blazing yule before us,
Fa la la la la, la la la la,
Strike the harp and join the chorus,
Fa la la la la, la la la la.
Follow me in merry measure,
Fa la la, la la la, la la la,
While I tell of yuletide treasure.
Fa la la la la, la la la la.

3. Fast away the old year passes,
Hail the new, ye lads and lasses,
Sing we joyous all together,
Heedless of the wind and weather.

12. O Come, All Ye Faithful

Music: John Francis Wade (1711–86)
English translation: Frederick Oakley (1802–80) and others
Arr. Barrie Carson Turner

At a moderate pace

*Notes in brackets for verse 1 only.

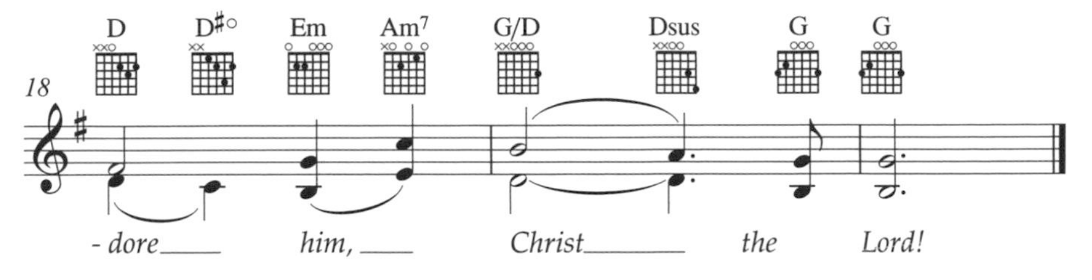

2. God of God,
   Light of Light,
Lo! he abhors not the Virgin's womb;
   Very God,
   Begotten, not created:
   O come let us adore him
   O come let us adore him,
   O come let us adore him,
   O come let us adore him,
   Christ the Lord!

3. See how the Shepherds,
   Summoned to his cradle,
Leaving their flocks, draw nigh with lowly fear;
   We too will thither
   Bend our joyful footsteps:

4. Lo! star-led chieftains,
   Magi, Christ adoring,
Offer him incense, gold and myrrh;
   We to the Christ Child
   Bring our heart's oblations:

5. Child, for us sinners
   Poor and in the manger,
Fain we embrace thee, with awe and love;
   Who would not love thee,
   Loving us so dearly?

6. Sing, choirs of Angels,
   Sing in exultation,
Sing, all ye citizens of heaven above;
   Glory to God
   In the Highest:

7. Yea, Lord, we greet thee,
   Born this happy morning,
Jesu, to thee be glory given;
   Word of the Father,
   Now in flesh appearing:

13. God Bless the Master of this House

(Furry Day Carol)

Music: Cornish traditional
Words: traditional
Arr. Barrie Carson Turner

Spirited and bright

2. Then let us all most merry be,
And sing with cheerful voice-a,
For we have good occasion now
This time for to rejoice-a.

The Saviour of all people
Upon this time was born-a,
Who did from death deliver us,
When we were left forlorn-a.

3. Then sing with voices cheerfully,
For Christ this time was born-a,
Who did from death deliver us
When we here left forlorn-a.

14. Silent Night!

Music: Franz Gruber (1787–1863)
Words: Original German by
Josef Mohr (1792–1848)
English translation anonymous
Arr. Barrie Carson Turner

Slowly

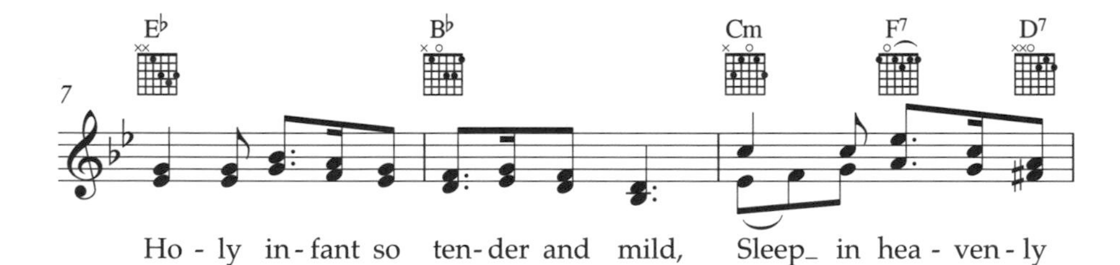

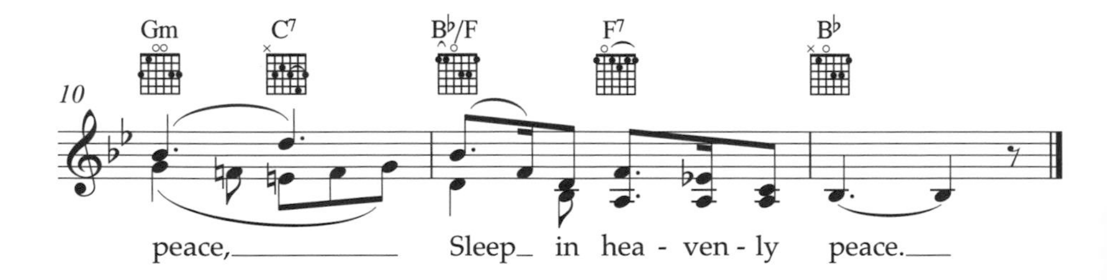

2. Silent night! Holy night!
   Shepherds wake at the sight:
   Glory streams from heaven afar,
   Heavenly hosts sing Alleluia:
   Christ the Saviour is born!
   Christ the Saviour is born!

3. Silent night! Holy night!
   Son of God, love's pure light;
   Radiance beams from thy holy face,
   With the dawn of redeeming grace,
   Jesus, Lord, at thy birth,
   Jesus, Lord, at thy birth.

15. O Little Town of Bethlehem

Music: English traditional
Words: Phillips Brooks (1835–93)
Arr. Barrie Carson Turner

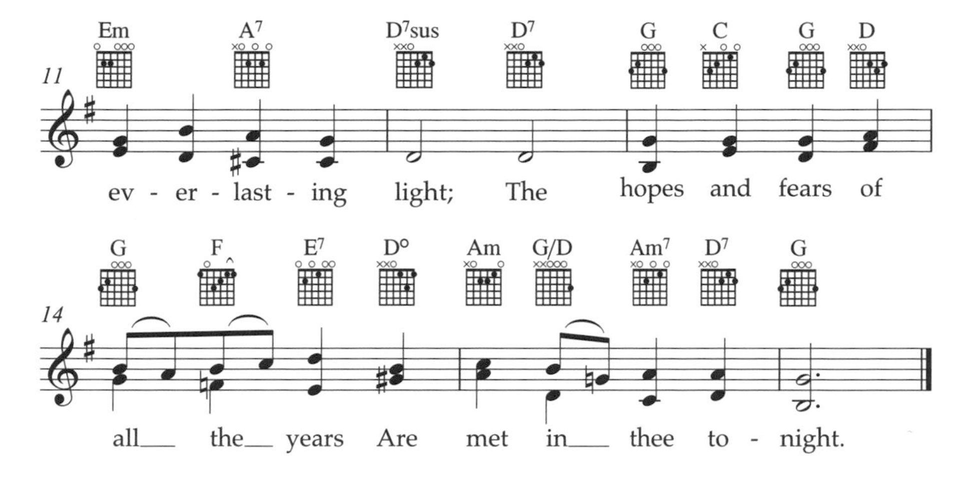

2. O morning stars, together
   Proclaim the holy birth,
   And praises sing to God the King,
   And peace to men on earth;
   For Christ is born of Mary;
   And, gathered all above,
   While mortals sleep, the angels keep
   Their watch of wondering love.

3. How silently, how silently,
   The wondrous gift is given!
   So God imparts to human hearts
   The blessings of his heaven.
   No ear may hear his coming;
   But in this world of sin,
   Where meek souls will receive him, still
   The dear Christ enters in.

4. O holy child of Bethlehem,
   Descend to us, we pray;
   Cast out our sin, and enter in,
   Be born in us today.
   We hear the Christmas Angels
   The great glad tidings tell:
   O come to us, abide with us,
   Our Lord Emmanuel.

16. Here We Come A-Wassailing

Words and Music: English traditional carol
Arr. Barrie Carson Turner

Cheerful, with movement

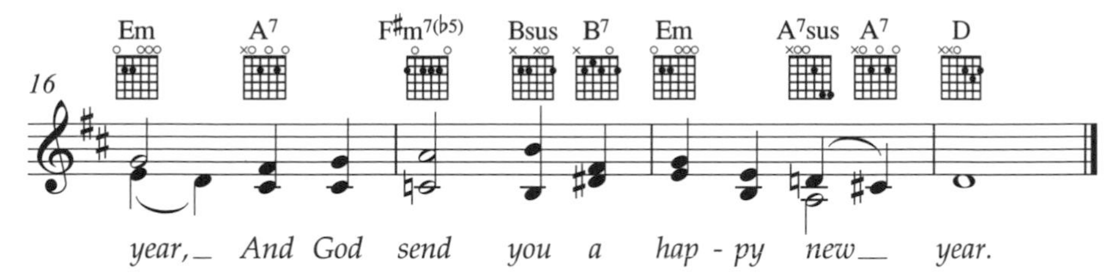

2. Our wassail cup is made
 Of the rosemary tree,
 And so is your beer
 Of the best barley.

 Love and joy come to you,
 And to you your wassail too
 And God bless you and send you
 A happy new year,
 And God send you a happy new year.

3. We are not daily beggars
 That beg from door to door,
 But we are neighbours' children
 Whom you have seen before.

4. Good master and good mistress,
 As you sit by the fire,
 Pray think of us poor children
 Who are wandering in the mire.

5. We have a little purse
 Made of ratching leather skin;
 We want some of your small change
 To line it well within.

6. Call up the butler of this house,
 Put on his golden ring;
 Let him bring us a glass of beer,
 And the better we shall sing.

7. Bring us out a table,
 And spread it with a cloth;
 Bring us out a mouldy cheese,
 And some of your Christmas loaf.

8. God bless the master of this house,
 Likewise the mistress too;
 And all the little children
 That round the table go.

17. O Christmas Tree

2. O Christmas tree, O Christmas tree!
   Thou hast a wondrous message!
   O Christmas tree, O Christmas tree!
   Thou hast a wondrous message!
   Thou dost proclaim the Saviour's birth,
   Goodwill to men and peace on earth.
   O Christmas tree, O Christmas tree!
   Thou hast a wondrous message!

18. Masters in this Hall

Music: French traditional carol tune
Words: William Morris (1834–96)
Arr. Barrie Carson Turner

Bright and brisk

2. Going o'er the hills,
   Through the milk-white snow,
   Heard I ewes bleat
   While the wind did blow:

   Nowell! Nowell! Nowell!
   Nowell sing we clear!
   Holpen are all folk on earth,
   Born is God's son so dear:
   Nowell! Nowell! Nowell!
   Nowell sing we loud!
   God today hath poor folk raised
   And cast a-down the proud.

3. Shepherds many an one
   Sat among the sheep,
   No man spake more word
   Than they had been asleep:

4. Quoth I, 'Fellows mine,
   Why this guise sit ye?
   Making but dull cheer,
   Shepherds though ye be?'

5. Shepherds should of right
   Leap and dance and sing
   Thus to see ye sit,
   Is a right strange thing':

6. Quoth these fellows then,
   'To Bethlem town we go,
   To see a mighty lord
   Lie in manger low':

7. 'How name ye this lord,
   Shepherds?' then said I,
   'Very God', they said,
   'Come from heaven high':

8. Then to Bethlem town
   We went two and two,
   And in a sorry place
   Heard the oxen low:

9. Therein did we see
   A sweet and goodly may
   And a fair old man,
   Upon the straw she lay:

10. And a little child
    On her arm had she,
    'Wot ye who this is?'
    Said the hinds to me:

11. Ox and ass let him know,
    Kneeling on their knee,
    Wondrous joy had I
    This little babe to see:

12. This is Christ the Lord,
    Masters be ye glad!
    Christmas is come in,
    And no folk should be sad:

19. Ceremonies for Christmas

Music: Old English air
Words: Robert Herrick (1591–1674)
Arr. Barrie Carson Turner

Bright and cheerful

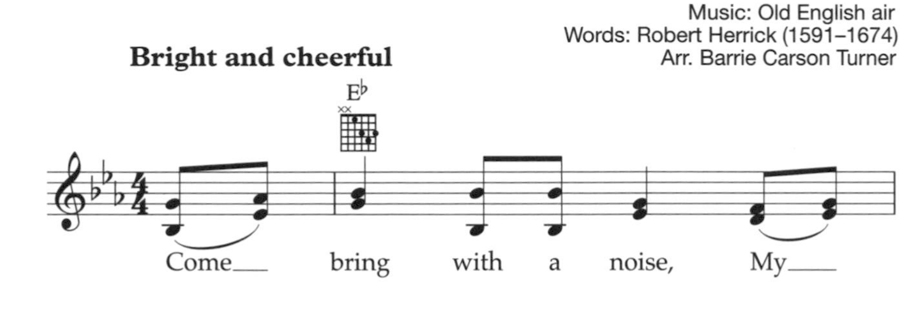

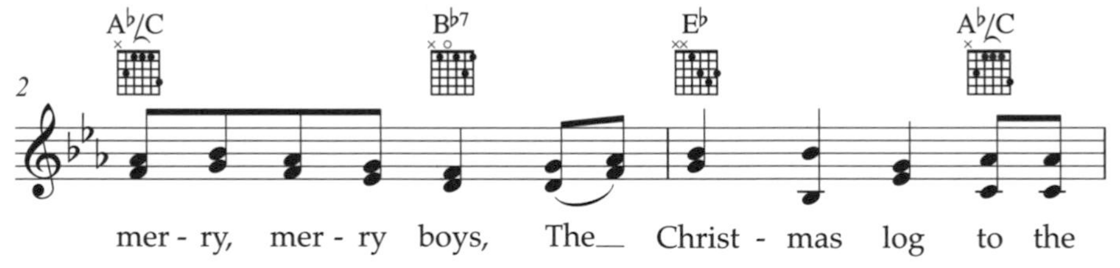

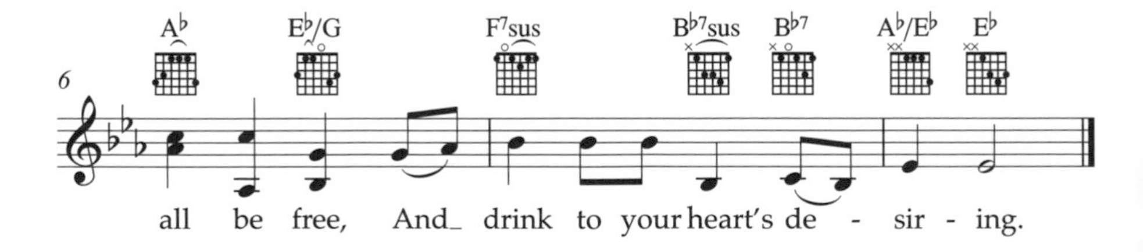

2. With last year's brand,
   Light the new block, and
   For good success in his spending,
   On your psalt'ries play
   That sweet luck may
   Come while the log is attending.

3. Now drink the strong beer,
   Cut the white loaf here,
   The while the meat is a-shredding,
   For the rare mince pie
   And the plums stand by
   To fill the paste that's a–kneading.

20. See Amid the Winter's Snow

Music: John Goss (1800–80)
Words: Edward Caswall (1814–78)
Arr. Barrie Carson Turner

Broad, with movement

G Am7 G/B Bm C G Em Am D7 G

See a - mid the win - ter's snow, Born for us on

4
A7 Dsus D G Am7 G/B Bm C G

earth be - low; See the ten - der Lamb ap - pears,

7
Em Am7(♭5) G/D Am Dsus D G Bm C G

Pro - mised from e - ter - nal years: *Hail, thou ev - er -*

10
Am D Bm(♭5) Eaug E7 Am A7 D

bless - èd morn; Hail, re - demp - tion's hap - py dawn;

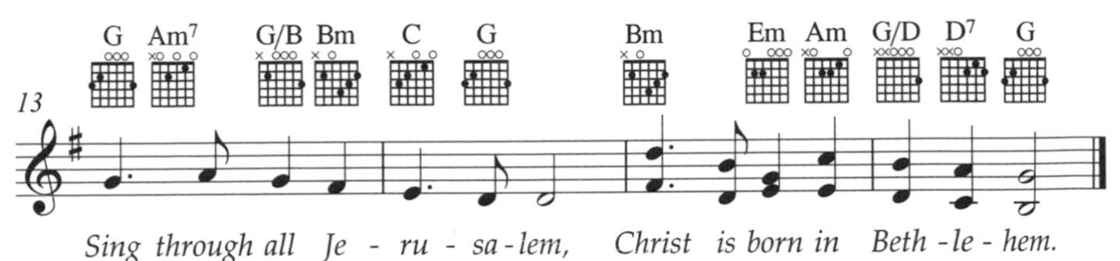

2. Lo, within a manger lies
He who built the starry skies;
He who throned in height sublime
Sits amid the cherubim:
Hail, thou ever–blessèd morn . . .

3. Say, ye holy shepherds, say
What your joyful news today;
Wherefore have ye left your sheep
On the lonely mountain steep?
Hail, thou ever–blessèd morn . . .

4. 'As we watched at dead of night,
Lo, we saw a wondrous light;
Angels singing "Peace on earth"
Told us of the Saviour's birth:'
Hail, thou ever–blessèd morn . . .

5. Sacred infant, all divine,
What a tender love was thine,
Thus to come from highest bliss
Down to such a world as this:
Hail, thou ever–blessèd morn . . .

6. Teach, O teach us, Holy Child,
By thy face so meek and mild,
Teach us to resemble thee,
In thy sweet humility.
Hail, thou ever–blessèd morn . . .

21. O Come, O Come, Emmanuel!

(Veni, veni, Emmanuel)

Music: Adapted from a plainchant by Thomas Helmore (1811–90)
Words: Latin 18th cent., trans. John Mason Neale (1818–66)
Arr. Barrie Carson Turner

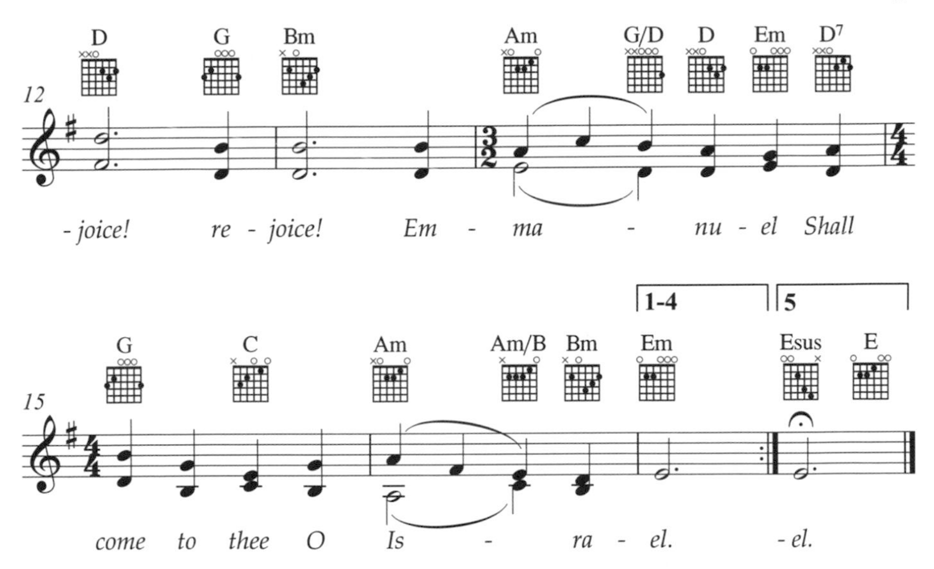

2. O come, thou Rod of Jesse, free
   Thine own from Satan's tyranny;
   From depths of hell thy people save,
   And give them victory o'er the grave.

   Rejoice! Rejoice! Emmanuel
   Shall come to thee, O Israel.

3. O come, thou Dayspring, come and cheer
   Our spirits by thine advent here;
   Disperse the gloomy clouds of night,
   And death's dark shadows put to flight.

4. O come, O come, thou Lord of Might,
   Who to thy tribes, on Sinai's height,
   In ancient times didst give the law
   In cloud, and majesty, and awe.

5. O come, thou Key of David, come,
   And span wide our heavenly home;
   Make safe the way that leads on high,
   And close the path to misery.

22. While Shepherds Watched their Flocks

Music: *Este's Psalter* (1592)
Words: Nahum Tate (1652–1715)
Arr. Barrie Carson Turner

Not too fast

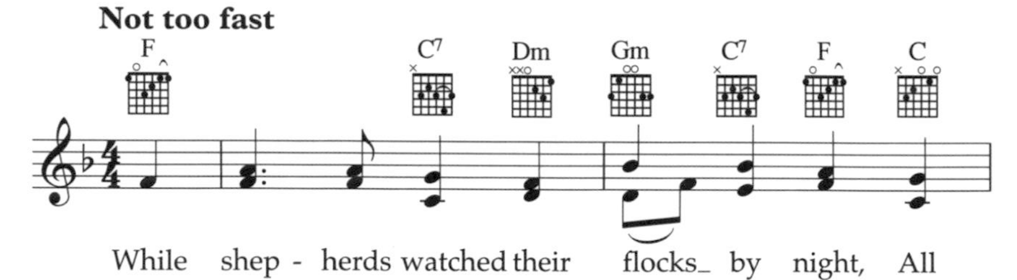

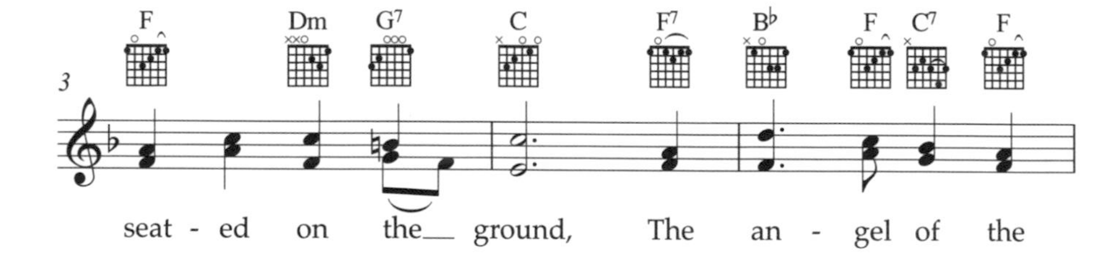

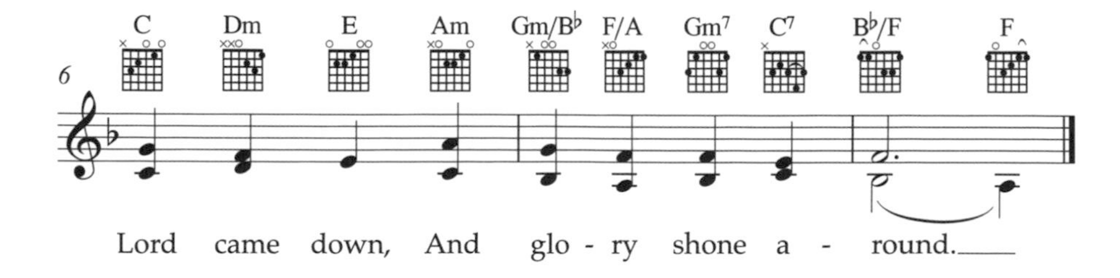

2. 'Fear not,' said he (for mighty dread
   Had seized their troubled mind);
'Glad tidings of great joy I bring
   To you and all mankind.

3. 'To you in David's town this day
   Is born of David's line
A Saviour, who is Christ the Lord;
   And this shall be the sign:

4. 'The heavenly Babe you there shall find
   To human view displayed,
All meanly wrapped in swathing bands,
   And in a manger laid.'

5. Thus spake the seraph; and forthwith
   Appeared a shining throng
Of angels praising God, who thus
   Addressed their joyful song:

6. 'All glory be to God on high,
   And to the earth be peace;
Goodwill henceforth from heaven to men
   Begin and never cease.'

23. Rejoice and be Merry

Words and Music: English traditional
Arr. Barrie Carson Turner

2. A heavenly vision appeared in the sky!
   Vast numbers of angels the shepherds did spy,
   Proclaiming the birthday of Jesus our King,
   Who brought us salvation his praises we'll sing.

3. Likewise a bright star in the sky did appear,
   Which led the wise men from the east to draw near;
   They found the Messiah, sweet Jesus our King,
   Who brought us salvation his praises we'll sing.

4. And when they were come, they their treasures unfold,
   And unto him offered myrrh, incense, and gold.
   So blessèd for ever be Jesus our King,
   Who brought us salvation his praises we'll sing.

24. The Holly and the Ivy

Words and Music: English traditional
Arr. Barrie Carson Turner

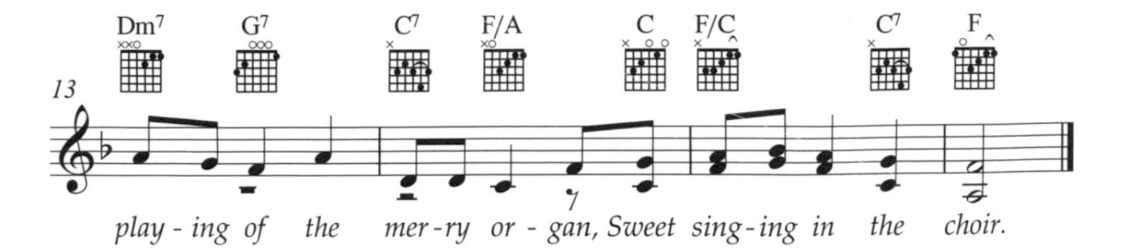

2. The holly bears a blossom,
   As white as the lily flower,
   And Mary bore sweet Jesus Christ
   To be our sweet Saviour:

   O the rising of the sun
   And the running of the deer,
   The playing of the merry organ,
   Sweet singing in the choir.

3. The holly bears a berry,
   As red as any blood,
   And Mary bore sweet Jesus Christ
   To do poor sinners good:

4. The holly bears a prickle,
   As sharp as any thorn,
   And Mary bore sweet Jesus Christ
   On Christmas Day in the morn:

5. The holly bears a bark,
   As bitter as any gall,
   And Mary bore sweet Jesus Christ
   For to redeem us all:

25. Rise up, Shepherd, an' Foller

Words and Music: Traditional American sprirtual
Arr. Barrie Carson Turner

Relaxed, but flowing tempo

E♭ A♭ E♭ Fm Cm B♭7 E♭

There's a star in the east on Christ - mas morn,

E♭ D♭ B♭7 E♭

Rise up, shep - herd, an' fol - ler; It will

E♭ A♭ E♭/G Fm Gm7 G♭7(♭5) F7 Fm7(♭5)

lead to the place where the Sa - viour's born,

E♭/B♭ Fm E♭ B♭7 E♭ A♭ B♭7 E♭ B♭

Rise up, shep - herd, an' fol - ler: Leave your sheep an'

A♭maj7 Fm E♭ E♭ D♭ B♭7 E♭ Cm7 F7(♭5)

leave your lambs, Rise up, shep - herd, an' fol - ler;

2. If you take good heed of the angel's words,
Rise up, shepherd, an' foller,
You'll forget your flocks, you'll forget your herds,
Rise up, shepherd, an' foller.
Leave your sheep an' leave your lambs,
Rise up, shepherd, an' foller,
Leave your ewes an' leave your rams,
Rise up, shepherd, an' foller.
Foller, foller,
Rise up shepherd, an' foller,
Foller the star of Bethlehem,
Rise up, shepherd, an' foller.

26. I Saw Three Ships

Words and Music: English traditional carol
Arr. Barrie Carson Turner

Moderately, with a lilt

G Am/G D^7/G Am/G

I saw three ships come sail - ing in, *On*

3

G Em A^7 D^7sus D^7

Christ - mas day On Christ - mas day, I

5

G Am G/D C G/B Am

saw three ships come sail - ing in *On*

7

G/D C | 1-8 D^7 G | 9 A^7 D^7 G

Christ - mas Day in the morn - ing 2. And *morn - ing.*

2. And what was in those ships all three?

3. Our Saviour Christ and his lady.

4. Pray, whither sailed those ships all three?

5. O, they sailed into Bethlehem.

6. And all the bells on earth shall ring.

7. And all the angels in Heaven shall sing.

8. And all the souls on earth shall sing

9. Then let us all rejoice amain!

27. Angels, from the Realms of Glory

Music: French traditional
English translation: J. Montgomery (1771–1854)
Arr. Barrie Carson Turner

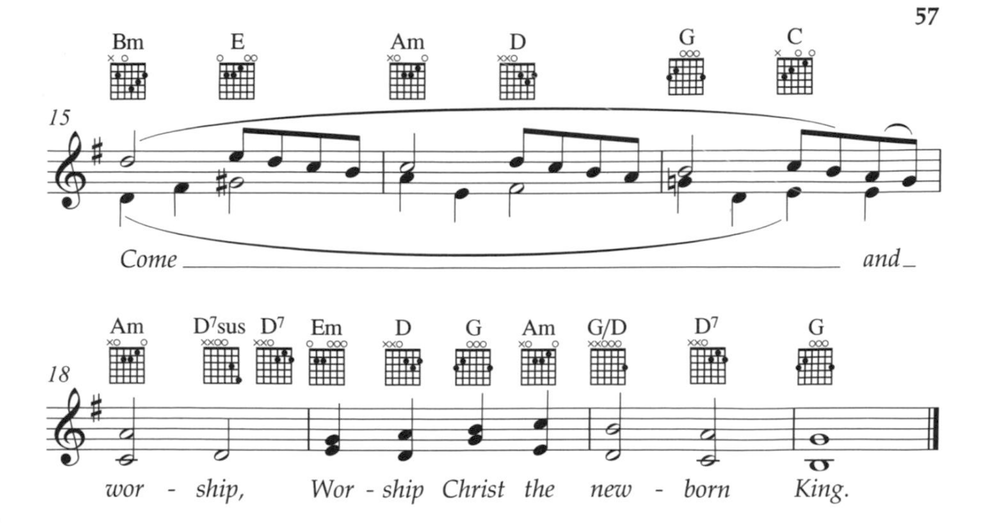

2. Shepherds in the field abiding,
   Watching o'er your flocks by night,
   God with man is now residing;
   Yonder shines the infant Light:

   Come and worship,
   Christ the new-born King;
   Come and worship,
   Worship Christ the new-born King.

3. Sages, leave your contemplations;
   Brighter visions beam afar;
   Seek the great Desire of Nations;
   Ye have seen his natal star:

4. Saints before the altar bending,
   Watching long in hope and fear,
   Suddenly the Lord, descending,
   In his temple shall appear:

5. Though an infant now we view him,
   He shall fill his Father's throne,
   Gather all the nations to him;
   Every knee shall then bow down:

28. Shepherds! Shake off your Drowsy Sleep

(Chantans! Bargies, Nové, Nové)

Music: Besançon Carol
Words: Anon.
Arr. Barrie Carson Turner

2. Hark! Even now the bells ring round,
   Listen to their merry sound,
   Hark! How the birds new songs are making
   As if winter's chains were breaking.

   Shepherds! The chorus come and swell!
   Sing Noel, oh sing Noel.

3. See how the flowers all burst anew,
   Thinking snow is summer dew;
   See how the stars afresh are glowing,
   All their brightest beams bestowing.

4. Cometh at length the age of peace,
   Strife and sorrow now shall cease;
   Prophets foretold the wondrous story
   Of this Heaven-born Prince of Glory.

5. Shepherds! Then up and quick away,
   Seek the Babe ere break of day;
   He is the hope of every nation,
   All in him shall find salvation.

29. We Three Kings of Orient Are

Words and Music: John Henry Hopkins (1820–91)
Arr. Barrie Carson Turner

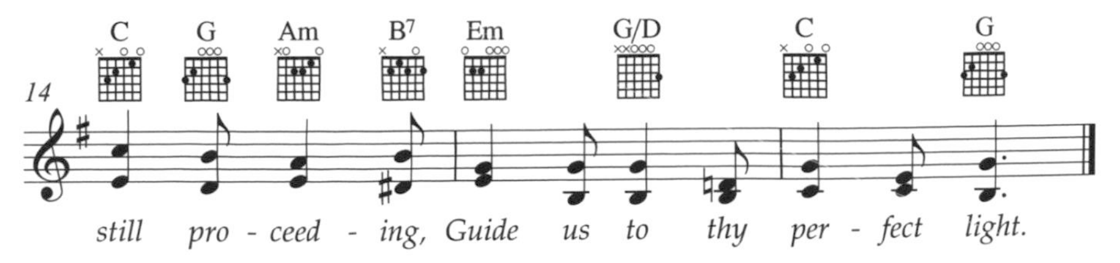

(Melchior)

2. Born a King on Bethlehem plain,
   Gold I bring, to crown him again–
   King for ever, ceasing never,
   Over us all to reign:

   O star of wonder, star of night,
   Star with royal beauty bright,
   Westward leading, still proceeding,
   Guide us to thy perfect light.

(Caspar)

3. Frankincense to offer have I;
   Incense owns a Deity nigh:
   Prayer and praising, all men raising,
   Worship him, God most high:

(Balthazar)

4. Myrrh is mine; its bitter perfume
   Breathes a life of gathering gloom;
   Sorrowing, sighing, bleeding, dying,
   Sealed in the stone-cold tomb:

(All)

5. Glorious now, behold him arise,
   King, and God, and sacrifice!
   Heaven sings alleluya,
   Alleluya the earth replies:

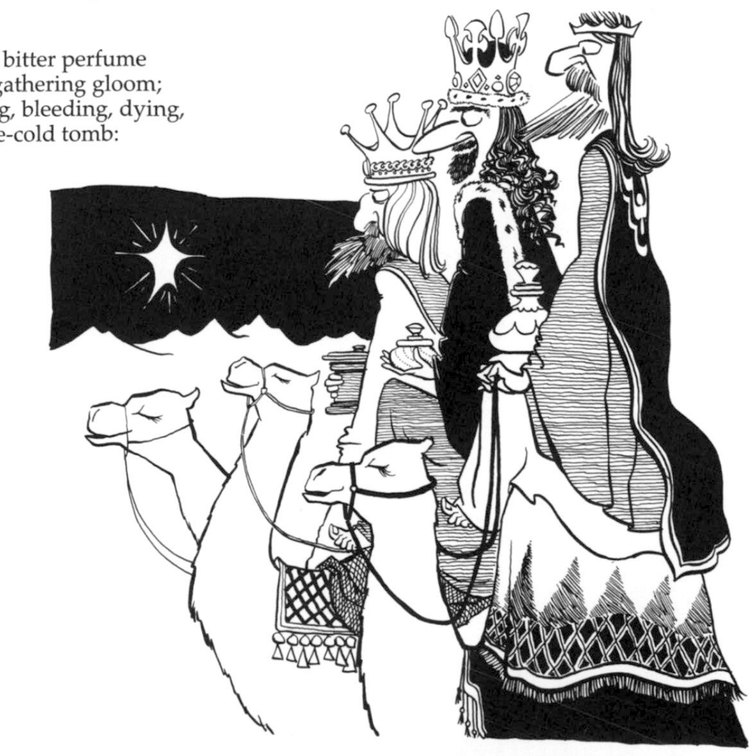

30. Shepherds, Rejoice

Music: French Carol tune
Words: Anon.
Arr. Barrie Carson Turner

Brisk and dance like

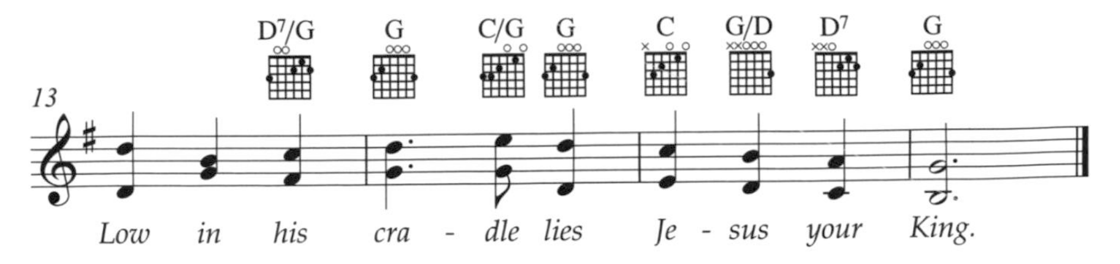

2. Mary her lovely babe lays to rest
   Folding his tender limbs close to her breast:

   Lullaby, lullaby, lullaby sing
   Low in his cradle lies Jesus your King.

3. Joyful as all now homewards depart,
   Cherish this scene of Christ's love in your heart.

31. Good Christian Men, Rejoice

Music: German, 14th century
English translation: John Mason Neale (1818–66)
Arr. Barrie Carson Turner

2. Good Christian men, rejoice
With heart and soul and voice!
Now ye hear of endless bliss,
Jesus Christ was born for this;
He hath ope'd the heavenly door,
And man is blessèd for evermore.
Christ was born for this!
Christ was born for this!

3. Good Christian men, rejoice
With heart and soul and voice!
Now ye need not fear the grave,
Jesus Christ was born to save,
Calls you one, and calls you all,
To gain his everlasting hall.
Christ was born to save!
Christ was born to save!

32. Tomorrow shall be my Dancing Day

Words and Music: English traditional
Arr. Barrie Carson Turner

With movement, dance like

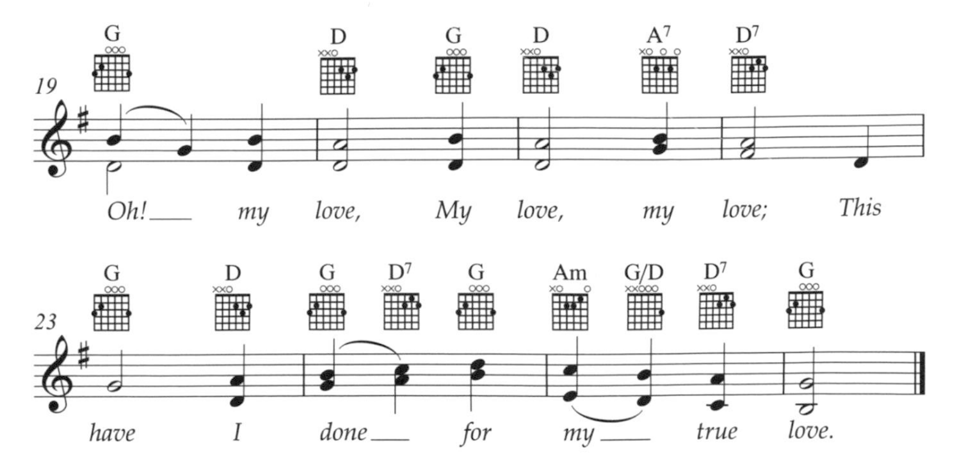

2. Then was I born of a Virgin pure,
   Of her I took my fleshly substance;
   Thus was I knit to Man's nature,
   To call my true love to the dance.

   Sing oh! my love,
   Oh! my love,
   My love, my love;
   This have I done for my true love.

3. In a manger laid and wrapp'd I was,
   So very poor, this was my chance,
   Betwixt an ox and a silly poor ass,
   To call my true love to my dance.

4. Then afterwards baptized I was,
   The Holy Ghost on me did glance,
   My father's voice heard from above,
   To call my true love to my dance.

5. Into the desert I was led,
   Where fasted I without substance;
   The devil bade me make stones my bread,
   To have me break my true love's dance.

6. The Jews on me they make great suit,
   And with me made great variance,
   Because they lov'd darkness rather than light
   To call my true love to my dance.

7. For thirty pence Judas me sold,
   His covetousness for to advance;
   Mark whom I kiss, the same do hold,
   The same is he shall lead the dance.

8. Before Pilate the Jews me brought,
   Where Barabbas had deliverance,
   They scourg'd me and set me at nought,
   Judged me to die to lead the dance.

9. Then on the cross hanged I was,
   Where a spear to my heart did glance,
   There issued forth both water and blood,
   To call my true love to my dance.

10. Then down to hell I took my way
    For my true love's deliverance,
    And rose again on the third day,
    Up to my true love to the dance.

11. Then up to heaven I did ascend,
    Where now I dwell in sure substance,
    On the right hand of God, that man
    May come unto the general dance.

33. We Wish You a Merry Christmas

Words and Music: West Country traditional
Arr. Barrie Carson Turner

2. We all want some figgy pudding,
   We all want some figgy pudding,
   We all want some figgy pudding,
   So bring some right here!

   Good tidings we bring
   To you and your kin;
   We wish you a merry Christmas
   And a happy New Year.

3. We won't go until we get some,
   We won't go until we get some,
   We won't go until we get some,
   So bring some right here!

34. The Coventry Carol

Music: English traditional
Words: From the *Pageant of the Shearmen and Tailors* (15th cent.)
Arr. Barrie Carson Turner

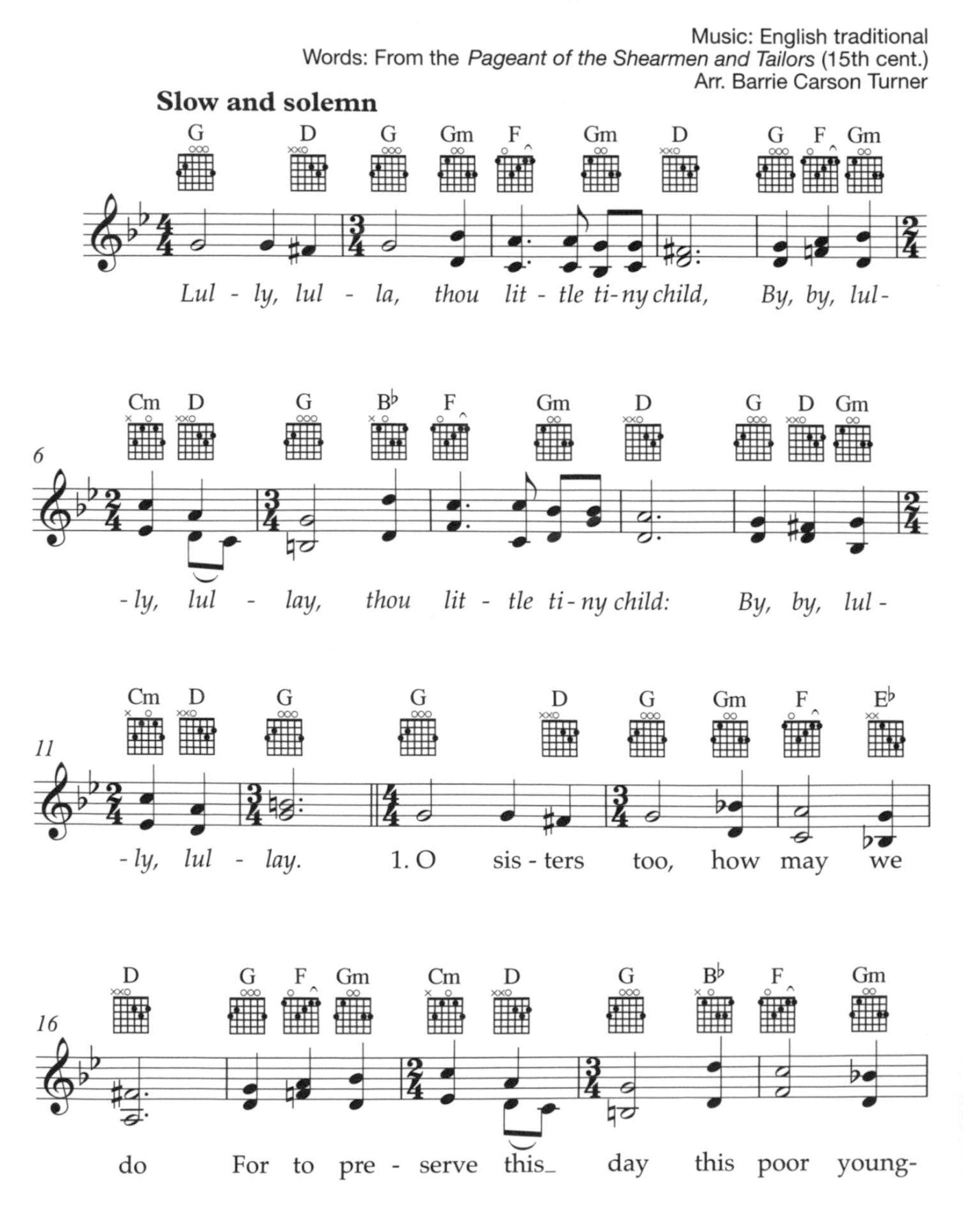

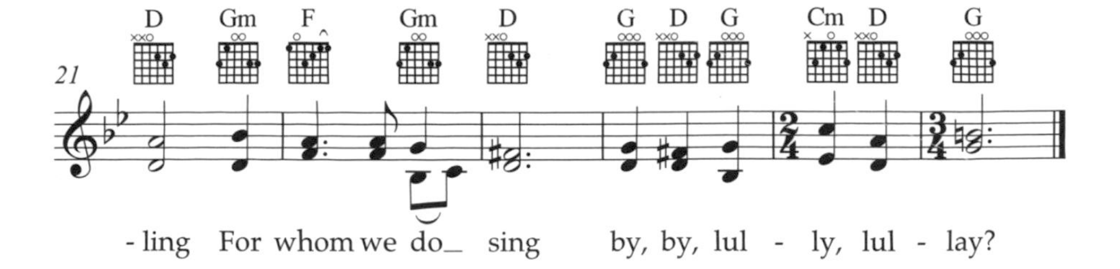

2. Herod the King, in his raging,
   Chargèd he hath this day his men of might,
   In his own sight all young children to slay.

3. That woe is me, poor child, for thee,
   And ever mourn and say: for thy parting
   Neither say nor sing by, by, lully, lullay.

35. Good King Wenceslas

Music: from *Piae Cantiones* (1582)
Words: John Mason Neale (1818–66)
Arr. Barrie Carson Turner

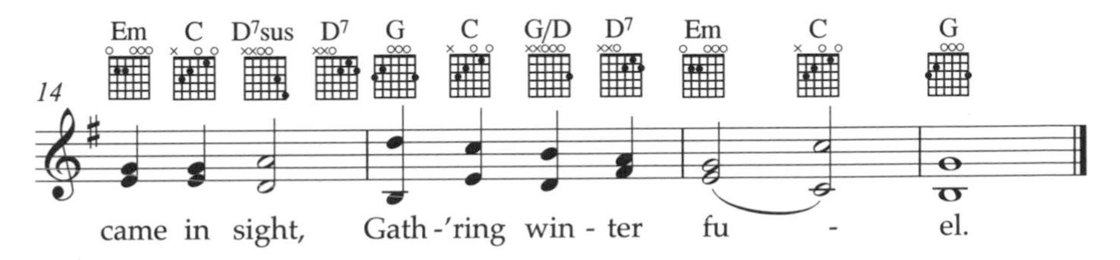

2. 'Hither, page, and stand by me,
   If thou know'st it, telling,
   Yonder peasant, who is he?
   Where and what his dwelling?'
   'Sire, he lives a good league hence,
   Underneath the mountain,
   Right against the forest fence,
   By Saint Agnes' fountain.'

3. 'Bring me flesh, and bring me wine,
   Bring me pine-logs hither:
   Thou and I will see him dine,
   When we bear them thither.'
   Page and monarch, forth they went,
   Forth they went together;
   Through the rude wind's wild lament
   And the bitter weather.

4. 'Sire, the night is darker now,
   And the wind blows stronger;
   Fails my heart, I know not how;
   I can go no longer.'
   'Mark my footsteps, good my page;
   Tread thou in them boldly:
   Thou shalt find the winter's rage
   Freeze thy blood less coldly.'

5. In his master's steps he trod,
   Where the snow lay dinted;
   Heat was in the very sod
   Which the Saint had printed.
   Therefore, Christian men, be sure,
   Wealth or rank possessing,
   Ye who now will bless the poor,
   Shall yourselves find blessing.

36. The Golden Carol

Words and Music: English traditional
Arr. Barrie Carson Turner

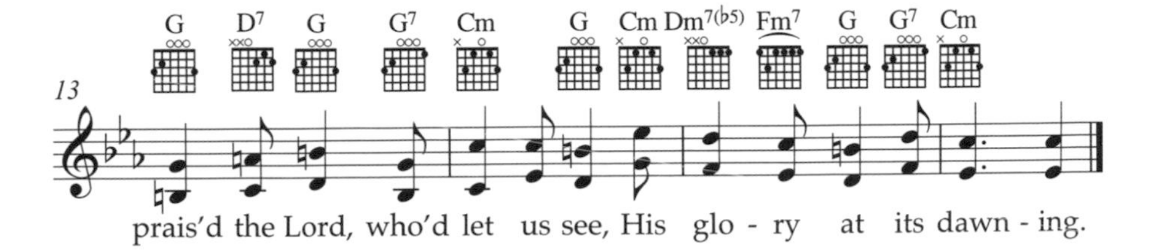

2. Oh! Ever thought be of his name,
   On Christmas in the morning,
   Who bore for us both grief and shame,
   Affliction's sharpest scorning.
   And may we die (when death shall come)
   On Christmas in the morning,
   And see in heav'n our glorious home,
   The star of Christmas morning.

37. God Rest You Merry, Gentlemen

Words and Music: English traditional
Arr. Barrie Carson Turner

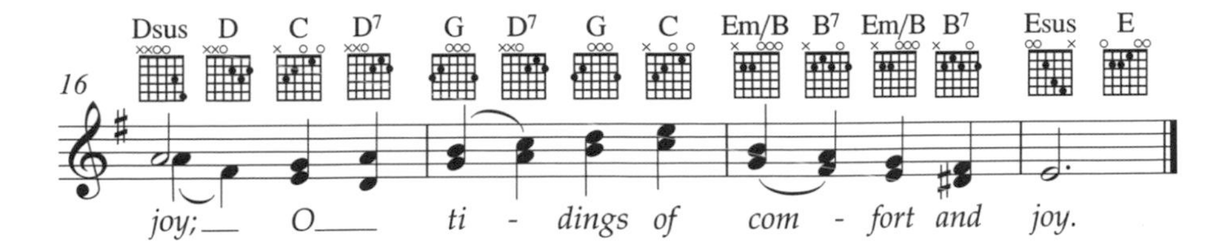

2. From God our heavenly Father
   A blessèd angel came,
   And unto certain shepherds
   Brought tidings of the same,
   How that in Bethlehem was born
   The Son of God by name:

   O tidings of comfort and joy,
   Comfort and joy;
   O tidings of comfort and joy.

3. The shepherds at those tidings
   Rejoicèd much in mind,
   And left their flocks a-feeding,
   In tempest, storm and wind,
   And went to Bethlehem straightway
   This blessèd babe to find:

4. But when to Bethlehem they came,
   Whereat this infant lay,
   They found him in a manger,
   Where oxen feed on hay;
   His mother Mary kneeling,
   Unto the Lord did pray:

5. Now to the Lord sing praises,
   All you within this place,
   And with true love and brotherhood
   Each other now embrace;
   This holy tide of Christmas
   All others doth deface:

38. The Infant King

(Oi! Betleem!)

Music: Basque Nöel
Words: S. Baring-Gould (1834-1924)
Arr. Barrie Carson Turner

Moderately, with a lilt

F C7 F C F Gm F/A B♭ F/A B♭

Sing lul - la - by! Lul - la - by ba - by, now re -

3

F/C C7 Dm C7 F B♭ Am B♭ C F/A G7 C G7

- clin - ing, Sing lul - la - by! Hush, do not wake the In - fant

6

C C7 F/A B♭ F/A Dm B♭

King. An - gels are watch - ing, stars are Shin - ing o - ver the

9

C/E E♭o G7 C7sus C7 F/A B♭ C7 F

place where he__ is ly - ing: Sing______ lul - la - by!

2. Sing lullaby!
   Lullaby baby, now a-sleeping,
   Sing lullaby!
   Hush, do not wake the Infant King,
   Soon will come bitter grief and weeping:
   Sing lullaby!

3. Sing lullaby!
   Lullaby baby, now a-dozing,
   Sing lullaby!
   Hush, do not wake the Infant King,
   Soon comes the cross, the nails, the piercing,
   Then in the grave at last reposing:
   Sing lullaby!

4. Sing lullaby!
   Lullaby! Is the babe a-waking?
   Sing lullaby!
   Hush, do not stir the Infant King
   Dreaming of Easter, gladsome morning,
   Conquering death, its bondage breaking:
   Sing lullaby!

39. Past Three O'Clock

Words and Music: English traditional
Arr. Barrie Carson Turner

Bright and rhythmic

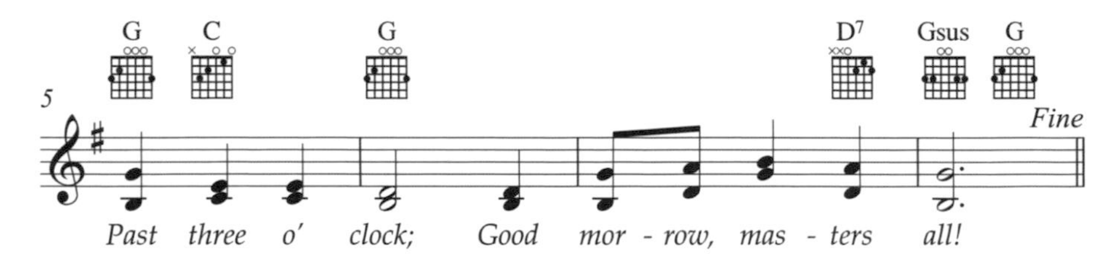

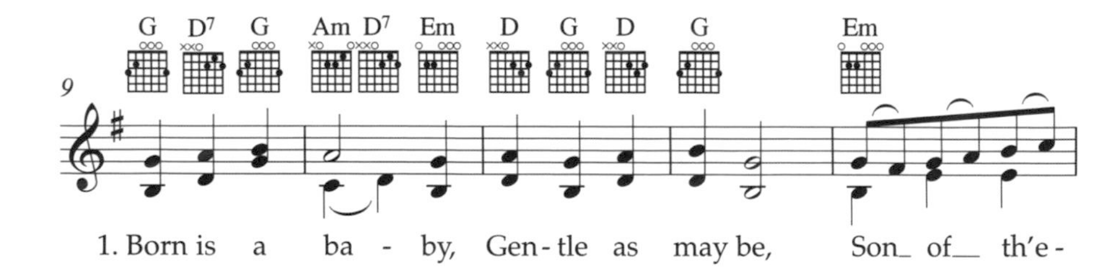

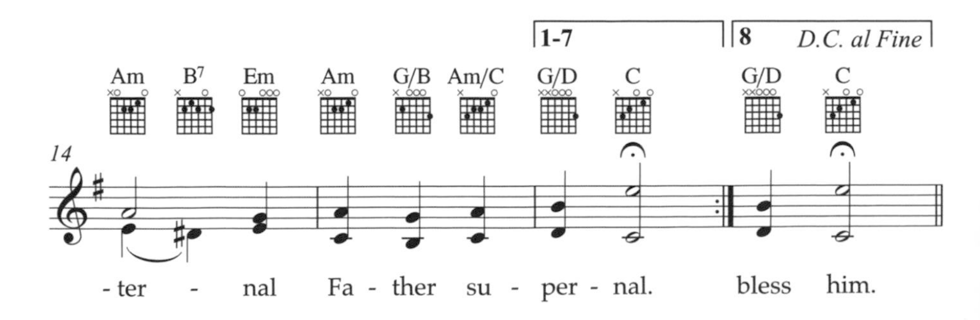

2. Seraph quire singeth,
   Angel bell ringeth:
   Hark how they rime it,
   Time it and chime it.

   Past three o'clock,
   And a cold and frosty morning;
   Past three o'clock;
   Good morrow, masters all!

3. Mid earth rejoices
   Hearing such voices,
   Ne'ertofore so well
   Carolling Nowell.

4. Hinds o'er the pearly
   Dewy lawn early
   Seek the high stranger
   Laid in the manger.

5. Cheese from the dairy
   Bring they for Mary,
   And, not for money,
   Butter and honey.

6. Light out of star-land
   Leadeth from far land
   Princes, to meet him,
   Worship and greet him.

7. Myrrh from full coffer,
   Incense they offer:
   Nor is the golden
   Nugget witholden.

8. Thus they: I pray you,
   Up, sirs, nor stay you
   Till ye confess him
   Likewise, and bless him.

40. The Moon Shines Bright

Words and Music: English traditional
Arr. Barrie Carson Turner

Moderately

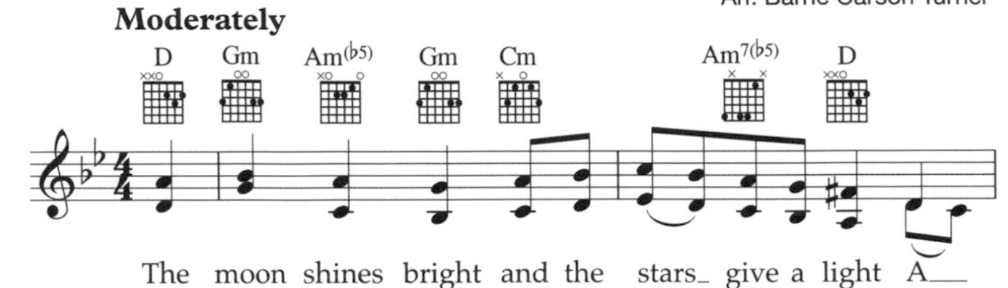

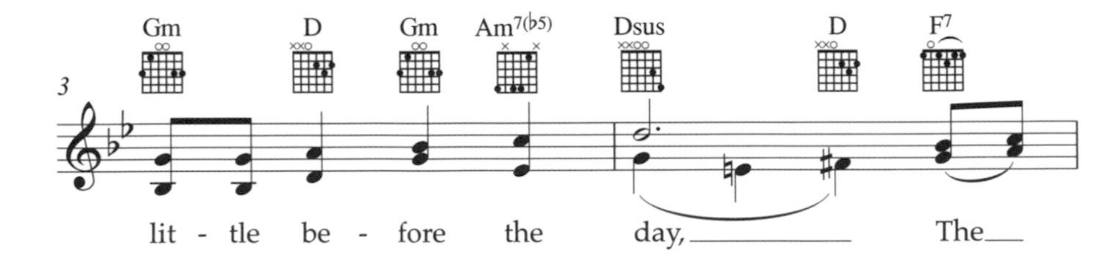

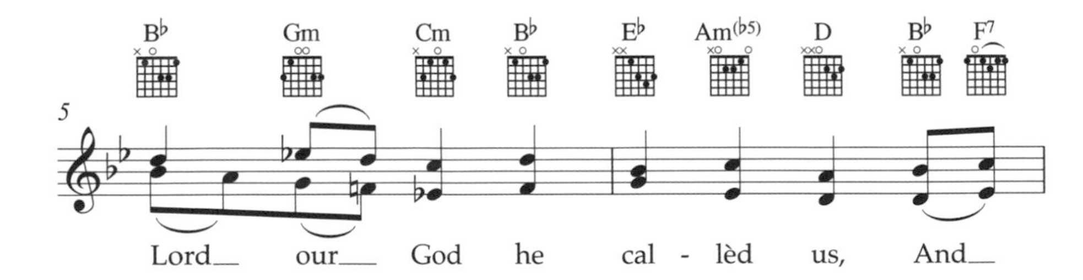

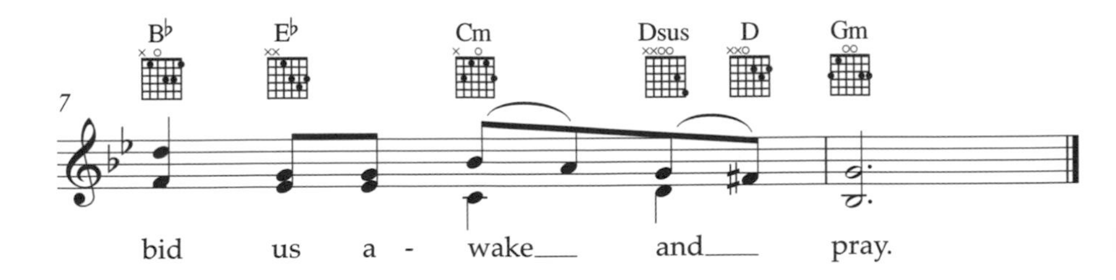

2. Awake, awake good people all,
   Awake and you shall hear,
   The Lord our God died on the cross,
   For us whom he loved so dear.

3. O fair, O fair Jerusalem,
   When shall I come to thee?
   When shall my sorrows have an end,
   Thy joy that I may see.

4. The fields were green as green could be
   When from his glorious seat
   The Lord, our God he blessèd us
   With his heavenly dew so sweet.

5. And for the saving of our souls
   Christ died upon the cross;
   We ne'er shall do for Jesus Christ
   As he has done for us.

6. The life of man is but a span
   And cut down in its flower;
   We are here today and tomorrow are gone,
   And we are dead in an hour.

7. My song is done, I must be gone,
   I can stay no longer here,
   God bless you all, both great and small,
   And send you a happy New Year.

41. Patapan

Music: Burgundian traditional
Arr. Barrie Carson Turner

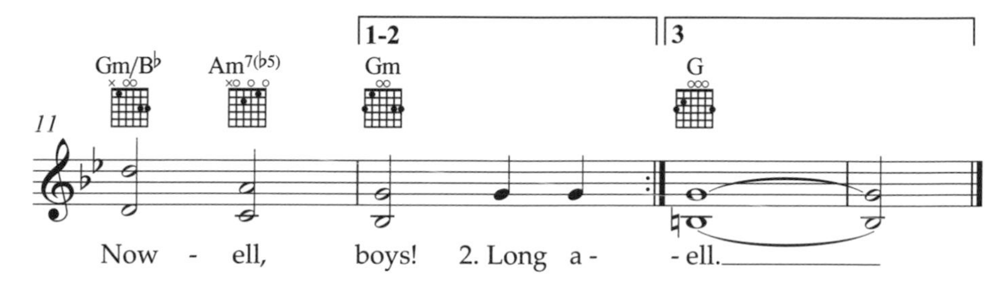

2. Long ago our fathers sang
   Such a song on this same day:
   'Twas of Bethlehem, their lay,
   Turelu-relu,
   Pata-patapan;
   Where wise kings and shepherds stray:
   To the stars their music rang.

3. As we join our choicest airs,
   In a hymn that upward fares:
   Earth and heaven seem near our prayers:
   Turelu-relu,
   Pata-patapan;
   Vanish all our daily cares
   While we dance and sing Nowell.

42. Brightest and Best of the Sons of the Morning

Music: J. F. Thrupp (1827–67)
Words: Reginald Heber (1783–1826)
Arr. Barrie Carson Turner

2. Cold on his cradle the dewdrops are shining;
   Low lies his head with the beasts of the stall;
   Angels adore him in slumber reclining,
   Maker, and Monarch and Saviour of all.

3. Say, shall we yield, him, in costly devotion,
   Odours of Edom, and offerings divine,
   Gems of the mountain, and pearls of the ocean,
   Myrrh from the forest, or gold from the mine?

4. Vainly we offer each ample oblation;
   Vainly with gifts would his favour secure;
   Richer by far is the heart's adoration;
   Dearer to God are the prayers of the poor.

5. Brightest and best of the sons of the morning,
   Dawn on our darkness, and lend us thine aid;
   Star of the east, the horizon adorning,
   Guide where our Infant Redeemer is laid.

43. The Angel Gabriel from Heaven Came

Music: Basque traditional
Words: S. Baring-Gould (1834–1924)
Arr. Barrie Carson Turner

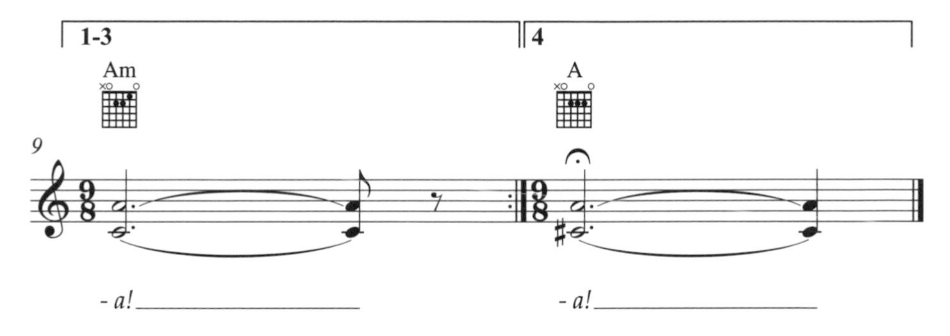

2. For known a blessèd Mother thou shalt be;
   All generation's laud and homour thee:
   Thy son shall be Emmanuel, by seers foretold.
   Most highly favoured lady! Gloria!

3. Then gentle Mary meekly bowed her head;
   'To me be as it pleaseth God!' she said.
   'My soul shall laud and magnify his holy name'.
   Most highly favoured lady! Gloria!

4. Of her, Emmanuel, the Christ, was born,
   In Bethlehem, all on a Christmas morn;
   And Christian folk throughout the world will ever say:
   Most highly favoured lady! Gloria!

44. Sans Day Carol

Words and Music: Traditional Cornish
Arr. Barrie Carson Turner

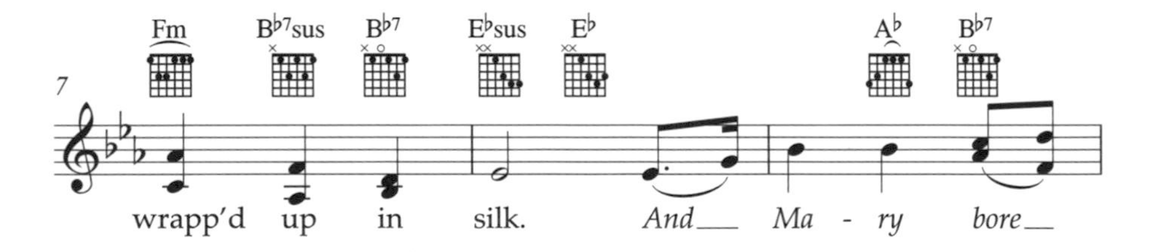

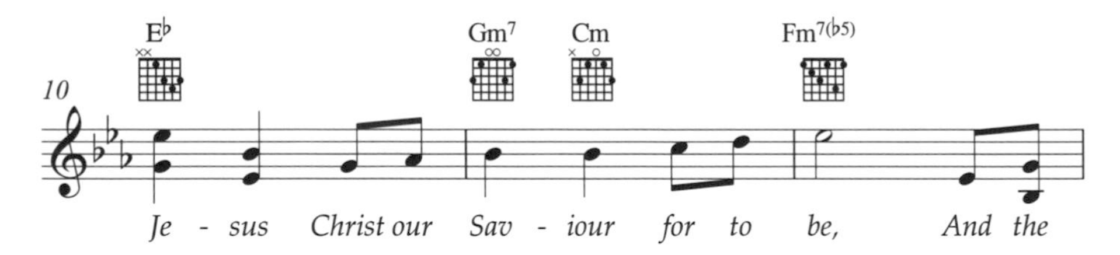

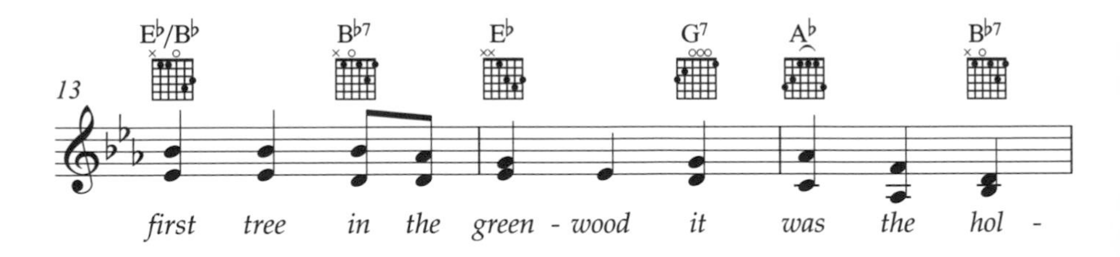

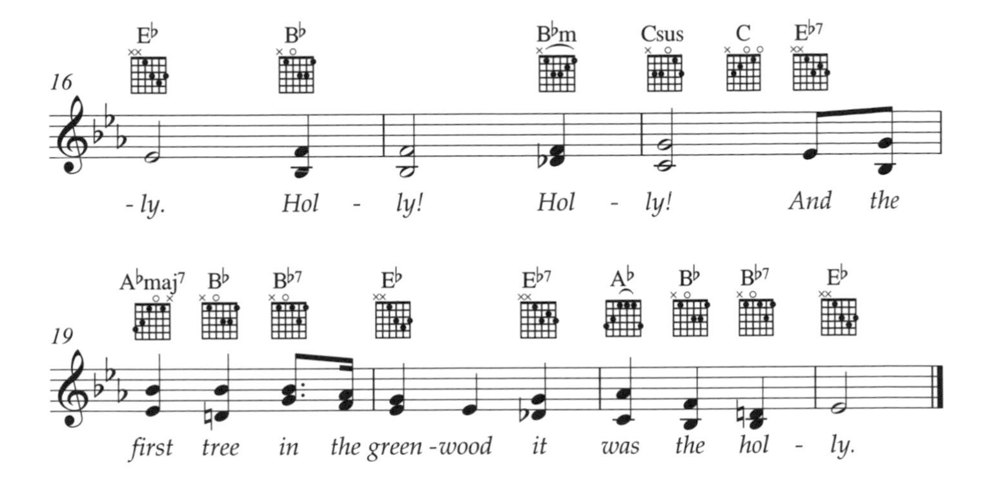

2. Now the holly bears a berry as green as the grass,
   And Mary bore Jesus, who died on the cross.

   And Mary bore Jesus Christ our Saviour for to be,
   And the first tree in the greenwood it was the holly.
   Holly! Holly!
   And the first tree in the greenwood it was the holly.

3. Now the holly bears a berry as black as the coal,
   And Mary bore Jesus, who died for us all.

4. Now the holly bears a berry as blood is it red,
   Then trust we our Saviour, who rose from the dead.

45. The Twelve Days of Christmas

Words and Music: Traditional
Arr. Barrie Carson Turner

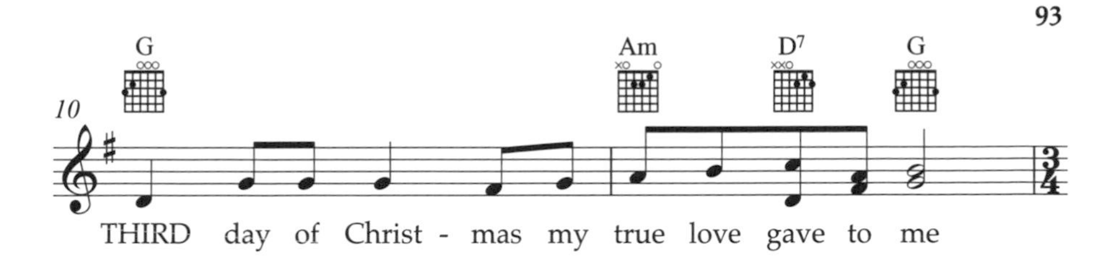
G Am D7 G
10
THIRD day of Christ - mas my true love gave to me

D D7
12
Three French_ hens, two tur - tle doves, and a

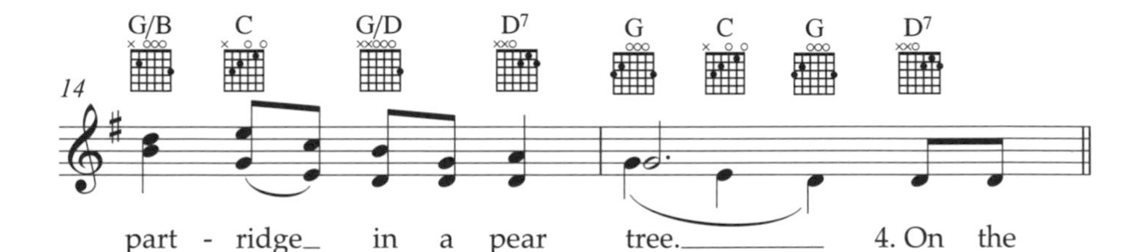
G/B C G/D D7 G C G D7
14
part - ridge_ in a pear tree._________ 4. On the

G Am D7 G
16
FOURTH day of Christ - mas my true love gave to me

D B♭ F7/C D/C
18
Four col - ly birds, three French_ hens, two tur - tle doves, and a

G/B C G/D D7 G B♭ D7/A
21
part - ridge in a pear tree. 5. On the
G Am D7 G
23
FIFTH day of Christ - mas my true love gave to me
D
25
Five gold rings, four col - ly birds, three French hens,
B♭ F7/C D/C G/B C G/D D7 G C G
28
two tur - tle doves, and a part - ridge in a pear tree. 6. On the
G Am D7 G
31
SIXTH
SEVENTH
EIGHTH
NINTH
TENTH
ELEVENTH
TWELFTH
day of Christ - mas my true love gave to me (- gave me)

D
Am7
D
G/D
D7
33
Six geese a - lay - ing, five gold_ rings, four col - ly birds,
Seven swans a - swim - ming,
Eight maids a - milk - ing,
Nine lad - ies danc - ing,
Ten lords a - leap - ing,
Eleven pip - ers pip - ing,
Twelve drum- mers drum- ming,
1-6
G7
C7
F7
B♭7
D/C
G/B
C
G/D
D7
36
three French_ hens, two tur - tle doves, and a part - ridge_ in a pear
7
rit.
slow
G
E♭7
D7
D7(♭5)
F7
B♭7
D7
39
D.𝄋
tree.___ 7. On the two tur - tle doves, and a
Tempo I
Bm7(♭5)
E+
E7
A7
D7sus
D7
G
G
A9(no root)
41
part - ridge_ in a pear tree.___

Index